Low Fee Socially Responsible Investing

Investing in Your Worldview on Your Terms

Tom Nowak, CFP®

Low Fee Socially Responsible Investing

Investing in Your Worldview on Your Terms

LCCN: 2012902119
ISBN: 1468033794
ISBN-13: 978-1468033793

DEDICATION

To my wife, Julie, and daughters, Brenna and Kendra,
who are my motivation to make the extra effort to work
towards a more sustainable world.

CONTENTS

ACKNOWLEDGMENTS

My sincere thanks to all who helped with their reviews, comments and support, including:

Susan Engle, Mary Erl, John Farrugia, Kathy Hankard, Mary Harris-King of CS2, Owen Moore (Cover Art), Julie Nowak, Margaret Carbonell Smith, and Robert Stanley

INTRODUCTION

This book contains guidance for building a customized stock portfolio that reflects your worldview. The portfolio can be developed, implemented and maintained inexpensively, with a minimum of professional assistance. If you have picked up this book, I assume that you are at least somewhat familiar with the concept of socially responsible investing, and may have read at least one of several good books that are available or have researched the topic online. The point of this book is not to present a comprehensive view of socially responsible investing (SRI) but, rather, to present to you my solution to a problem that I have spent the last few years trying to solve. I have shared the problem and solution with a number of investors and advisors, and have received an enthusiastic response. I would like to now share this story and solution with you.

Like many investors and investment advisors, I had enough reasons to put the idea of socially responsible investing aside. Until investigation proved otherwise, the typical misconceptions of poor return and lack of diversification were enough to justify caution. As an hourly, fee-only advisor the two most problematic areas to me were that the fees could be high and that, at the end of the day, how I could assure my clients (or myself) that they were at least investing according to their worldview. As I studied this area of investing more closely, I became aware of several solutions that came close to solving these problems.

There is information publicly available for well over 250 socially responsible mutual funds (e.g. **www.ussif.org**). Although I found this information helpful in making it clear which of the established social screens were used for each fund and what each fund charged investors to implement the model, I sensed something more was needed.

Not surprisingly, I found that socially responsible investing was of stronger interest to clients with a faith-based motive, or who viewed socially responsible investing as an area where they could express their views by avoiding investment in companies that they perceived as bad actors.

The roots of SRI are, indeed, with faith-based investing and it is relatively easy, in many cases, for individuals or advisors to identify a mutual fund that is designed to be consistent with their faith (e.g. there are funds for Christians of various denominations and for followers of Islam). Additionally, numerous funds that are secular in nature screen for one or more of the following criteria: environment, social, governance, and product category.

All things considered and upon close scrutiny, it is possible to find an investment approach for most investors that will not be much more costly than the typical actively managed, non-SRI, mutual fund (about 1 percent per year). But still, I had a problem or two.

One faith-based group I wanted to serve in the area of SRI does not yet have a mutual fund that screens in an area important to them. Like many faiths, members of the Baha'i Faith would be expected to have an interest in excluding investments in alcohol and tobacco, and would be interested in essentially the entire list of other established SRI screens. For Baha'is, the ideal company would also adhere to a principle of non-partisanship and would not support any candidate for political office. Since the majority of companies actively support partisan politics, a "relatively best in class" company would at least agree to fully disclose their political activities publicly. Unfortunately, however, non-partisanship and political disclosure have not yet become generally recognized SRI screens.

I could not find an established mutual fund that screened for corporate involvement in partisan politics. In 2010, I went from booth to booth at a national SRI conference and, quite frankly, was surprised to find that no one appeared to be using this criteria even though there is an increasing level of fund management activism on the subject via support of shareholder resolutions. As you might expect, when I began to discuss this additional criteria with mutual fund representatives, other advisors and investors, I found that a screen for political involvement would go well beyond a faith-based motive, and that many recognized the benefit of screening investments along this line. They saw that this screen would represent a potential safety factor, in that a company that feels it does not have to "pay to play" could be viewed as having stronger confidence in its products or services, and be less vulnerable to political payback (or retribution).

My first approach was to consider establishing a mutual fund using the services of a firm that could provide all of the regulatory and logistical support. This would not work well for my one-person investment advisory practice, however, as it would require an initial investment of at least $30,000 and annual expenses of about the same amount. I would have to rapidly attract many millions of dollars to offer the fund at an investment expense that I would be comfortable with (for me comfort, is getting the investor's investment expense very, very low).

Another potential solution was to refer clients to a portfolio development and asset management shop to generate, implement and maintain a custom portfolio. Again, to attract the right talent to the task, this approach still involved fees that would be no lower than the average actively-managed mutual fund. Also, it would put me in a position of being a salesperson in order to raise a critical amount of assets that were not mine. For a large account size, there is always the possibility of achieving a negotiated fee that might be acceptable; however, there are still many investors with smaller sized accounts that they want to put into an SRI strategy.

"Okay," you may ask at this point, "what is the problem with the typical 1% or higher annual asset management fee?" Well, for one, the title of this book includes the phrase "low fee." The first chapter of this book will make it clear why I have such a fee phobia and want you to at least be cautious in this area.

Having exhausted solutions that could be outsourced to others, I considered what I might be able to do to construct a customized, low fee, SRI portfolio that my clients could implement with little ongoing assistance. There did not appear to be a perfect solution in sight. After some trial and error, however, a very good solution emerged.

When taking an analytical approach to a problem, it is often necessary to experiment rather than rely solely on theory. It is also important to look as objectively as possible at what is fact and what is wishful thinking. Fortunately, there are portfolio development tools that allow for experimentation with hypothetical rather than real dollars. The fourth and fifth chapters of this book describe the rationale and development of the customized low fee portfolio approach. The other remaining chapters illustrate how you and a "low-net-fee" financial advisor can implement the strategy so that you can invest in accordance with your worldview.

The primary goal in publishing this book is to help make SRI accessible to a wider range of investors. My experience as an hourly, fee-only, financial planner is that there are many investors who want to participate more actively in how their money is invested. Also, once they become aware of the fees they have often been paying for financial services, they see the benefit of more active participation: in effect, the benefits of "sweat equity," whether it is filling out an account application themselves, working with a discount broker versus a full-service broker or working with a financial advisor on an hourly, as-needed, basis. For those of you interested in fully delegating investment decisions regarding your money, the information provided is intended to help you determine the value you are receiving for the fees you are paying.

My belief is that it would be great if more dollars were invested with social screening in mind. Even though we all have somewhat different perspectives, I do not believe that the impact of such activity will be canceled out. I believe the net effect will be to encourage companies that are dependent upon investor capital to become better actors, if for no other reason than to keep their relative cost of capital (i.e. money) low. That is to say, if investors are attracted to a company exhibiting exemplary social responsibility, they are willing to pay more for the stock (equity) and accept a lower interest rate for loans to them (bonds).

Disclaimer

This book contains guidance on how to build a customized stock portfolio that reflects your worldview with a minimum of professional assistance, and can be implemented and maintained inexpensively. You should treat the contents of this book as you would a sharp pair of scissors: if used carefully, you may be able to cut your investment costs substantially and produce satisfying results. If you are an inexperienced investor and use this book without at least a few hours of professional guidance, you may hurt yourself financially. We all have unique financial circumstances and prior investment knowledge. The suggestions of this book are not to be treated as specific investment, tax or legal advice.

Any references to investment performance are historical in nature. Past performance does not guarantee future results, and all investments entail risk of loss, including the potential for loss of principal. Each investor is unique, and factors including his or her investment experience, tax situation, time horizon, tolerance for risk and fluctuations in value should be weighed carefully before making an investment decision. Mutual funds are sold by prospectus only, and the investor should carefully review the current prospectus for any fund considered before investing.

The views expressed in this book are solely those of the author and do not necessarily represent the views of any organization that the author is associated with. The author does not receive any fees for mention of any source of information or service provider. The data and calculations represent the author's best effort to be fair and accurate, however no guarantee is made.

CHAPTER 1

INVESTMENT FEES: HIGH, MEDIUM & LOW

As with social screening criteria, the definition of what is an appropriate or acceptable investment fee is also somewhat dependent upon one's point of view. It seems logical that, if investment fees and service levels are fully disclosed, it should be relatively straightforward for investors to choose which service model best fits their need. Unfortunately, there are no consistent and clear rules across the financial services industry regarding fee disclosure, and investors often have to rely on their instincts as to what is fair and appropriate for them.

The primary objective of this book is to illustrate a low fee approach to SRI investing. It is therefore necessary that you, the reader, have good information about how to determine what is fair and appropriate. Although financial service providers may (and probably will) argue to the end of time as to which delivery model is best, I believe you can figure out which one is best for you with some effort. The math requirements to do so are simple   addition, subtraction, division and multiplication.   I would recommend a calculator, however, since some of the numbers can get pretty big.

In addition to the fees paid, directly or indirectly, for your investments themselves it is to your benefit to take the time to understand how investment brokers and advisors are paid, since these fees apply outside the area of SRI investing as well. This will also provide you an insight into what bias your broker or advisor may have in making recommendations.

There are three main ways that financial service providers get paid:

- by a commission (a sales charge, often a "front-end load" based on a percentage of the amount of money initially invested with them, or a "back-end load" charged when you sell the investment)

- by a percentage of assets under management (the typical range is between 0.25% and 2.0% of money being managed)

- an hourly rate (typically between $100 and $400 per hour, typically independent of the amount of assets under management).

A transportation analogy may help you appreciate the differences. A transportation model is particularly helpful since, like financial planning and investing, the objective is to get you safely from point A to some destination point B. The financial destination is that of independence from wage income.

The lowest fee approach for transportation is to drive your own car, perform all routine maintenance yourself and keep your travel destinations limited to the maps you have in your glove compartment and directions provided by friends and family members. Many do-it-yourselfers (DIY) use this strategy in their financial lives, as they do not utilize financial planners or investment advisors. If they spend the additional time reading a combination of at least one monthly personal finance magazine, articles published by one or two personal finance journalists, and some of the better books on investing, they have a fair chance of making the adjustments needed to safely reach their destination as long as life does not get too complicated. Unfortunately, however, there is certainly a large risk if investors misjudge the complexity of their situation or are unaware of lost opportunities. Picture a situation where a simple repair could have improved gas mileage or vehicle longevity, or where a global positioning system (GPS) could have saved a lot of time. Many investors utilize this approach, often fearing being sold services or products that they will regret. It is my experience that this fear is, unfortunately, well-founded.

A slightly more costly strategy than a drive-and-maintain-yourself approach is to seek the services of a certified mechanic on an as-needed or periodic basis. Additionally, to assure that you more easily arrive at your destination, the mechanic proposes installing a customized GPS system that is matched to the destinations you have in mind. In financial services, this would be a fee-only advisor paid on an hourly basis or a retainer fee based primarily on the number of service hours anticipated. This provides the flexibility to match the price paid for advice and service to the complexity of your personal financial circumstances. You are informed that the initial fee to install the customized GPS may be up to a few thousand dollars (for relatively simple situations, the initial fee may be much lower), but the annual maintenance is typically much less than one thousand dollars per year. As with obtaining general vehicle servicing, you are in a position to assess the value that is to be delivered prior to the start of work. Although this would appear to be a nearly ideal option for most investors, it is my best guess that this is, by far, the least used option of the four being presented. It is probably the least used because it is the least known-about service model and, perhaps, because it requires more self-accountability on the part of the investor than the remaining two models. When an investor refuses to implement agreed upon steps and follow ups, it is as if they pay for a customized GPS system but do not bother turning it on.

So, we are once again pondering our choices of getting to our desired destination. Driving our own car is getting to be too bothersome, so we decide to employ a limousine service to handle most of our driving (we still drive to the bank to cash a few checks and buy a couple of CDs, but that is about it). We begin to appreciate the benefits of sitting in the back seat of a beautifully appointed and maintained car, reading the paper or relaxing, and believe all is well since the limo driver has given us the impression that we could afford his services on, essentially, a permanent basis. As you might guess, this financial service model is becoming increasingly popular. The assets under management (AUM) model or percentage of assets (% annual fee) model typically costs between 1% and 2% of investable assets. Unlike the first two, more basic, choices (DIY and hourly), a common minimum fee is $5,000 per year to contract this level of service (e.g. 1% of $500,000 = $5,000 per year).

Is $5,000 per year a good value for having someone manage an investible net worth of $500,000? Is $10,000 per year a good value for a $1,000,000 nest egg? I will say more about that later.

What if we do not have enough resources to contract a limousine service? Let us keep the car in the garage for the same reasons noted earlier and hire a taxi. There is nothing to stop us from putting the taxi dispatcher on speed dial and keeping the car in the garage for all but trips to the credit union. In an effort to diversify, maybe we will even use a few different taxi services so we can ditch one of them if a driver gets too obnoxious or gets us lost too often. The taxi company does not tell us that we cannot afford their services in the long term, as they are compensated by the immediate fare. In the financial services area, this is the commission model, where a basic upfront fare of 5% on the amount invested is often charged, along with a meter that clicks along at 1% of your account value per year. This model is the most popular in usage. It represents the historical brokerage model and is typically available from large brokerage houses, broker-dealers that operate within banks and credit unions, and insurance companies. Like taxis, they are handy - and sometimes all you have to do is raise your hand and one comes along. Calculating the value obtained for this option, again, is dependent upon the size of your asset base. If you do not change investments too often and receive good service, the initial upfront fee could be a good value.

In my experience, too many investors come to me after realizing that they have been paying too much for the services they are receiving.

Again, there is an ongoing debate as to what fee structure is best for the investor. I would like to present some examples that may be helpful in allowing you to determine what is best for you. Keep in mind that this mathematical exercise will be important for you, as the investment approach that I will be presenting will require most of you to use an investment advisor. My examples will illustrate how each fee model could work.

An essential element of determining which fee structure works best for your needs is defining the amount of service you need and/or expect. If you fill out account applications online and make all investment selections without any assistance, you should be rewarded with a minimal amount of investment fees. On the other hand, if you require more comprehensive services, you should expect to pay a fair price for the service being provided. An example of comprehensive services might be initial and quarterly meetings with an advisor to review all of the important aspects of personal finance relevant to you - such as insurance needs, budgeting advice, tax advice, estate planning, implementation of investment advice, ongoing monitoring of the investments, and trading activity that meets the agreed-upon objectives.

For the purposes of this book, I would like to define "low fee" as an annual investment cost of less than 0.5% per year at a service level where both investment advice and annual net management fees are included.

In order to put "low fee" in perspective, it may be helpful to look at the distribution of mutual fund fees. Using Morningstar® - November 2011 data , a screen of SRI mutual funds in the database yielded the following breakdown:

Table 1

Annual Charge	Percentage of Funds (approx.)
0.5% or less	4 %
Between 0.5% and 1.0%	25 %
Between 1.0 and 1.2%	18 %
Between 1.2% and 2.0%	42 %
Between 2.0% and 3.0%	10 %
Greater than 3.0%	1%

At this point, it may be helpful to review the impact of annual investment expenses so that you may be better able to form your position on this important topic. Table 1 illustrates that the median expense ratio is between 1.2% and 2.0% per year for ongoing mutual fund investment management (i.e. excluding fees that may be due to commissions or secondary advisor fees).

Your first thought may be that an annual expense ratio is not very important provided the fund's performance, over fees, consistently exceeds the relevant benchmark. This is, of course, true. If your view in this particular area is that you are more likely to exceed benchmark performance if you pay higher fees, I suggest you examine the evidence by reading some of the wonderful books on the subject by Jack Bogle (the founder of Vanguard®), Larry Swedroe and Rick Ferri, all champions of a scientific or evidence-based view of investing (see Bibliography). You might find it interesting that the funds associated with annual fees over 3.0% in Table 1 had lackluster performance histories, while some of the funds with annual fees less than 0.5% had very good performance histories. If your view is that there is an association between low investment fees and higher performance, your position is validated by numerous books and publications.

Fortunately, most of us do not have to beat the market averages to meet our goals and, in any event, should not count on identifying an active fund manager who will exceed the benchmarks in the long term. If you would like to read a simple but convincing academic study on this topic, I recommend that you read the paper by Nobel Laureate William Sharpe referenced at the end of this book. Again, it is not impossible to outperform the benchmark in the long term, just very unlikely.

But let us keep in mind that, besides low fees, we are also talking about socially responsible investing. If your investing preferences mandate a very selective screening process that requires a great amount of ongoing diligence, performance is a secondary consideration. Development and maintenance of a very selective process with very active day-to-day management should be expected to be expensive. In such a case, you may not be able to identify a low fee option. You will find, however, that much depends upon the amount of money you have to invest. In that case, you may want to continue reading and see what might work best for you.

If there were not any alternatives to paying an average of approximately 1.2 percent for a diversified portfolio of socially screened investments, the story would end here with, perhaps, a recommendation that you study the available mutual funds, look at their track records and overall suitability to meet your needs. Fortunately, there are other alternatives. You could identify an advisor who is willing and able to work with you to develop a set of stock screens that are consistent with your worldview and will help you implement the model portfolio generated. There are currently established firms that can deliver this service for a fee that would be competitive with the established mutual fund average, provided the amount of assets you have to invest are significant (typically one million dollars or more).

As noted in the introduction, I wanted to determine what approach might be used to drive the investment cost down (noting again, the association between performance and investment fees). Chapter four introduces an approach that can significantly reduce the asset minimum and management fees.

In order to gain additional perspective on mutual fund costs, it may be helpful to look at this from the service provider perspective. As noted in the introduction, based on my investigation to date, it costs an investment advisor a minimum of approximately $30,000 to have a fund established, and ongoing basic expenses would be expected to be approximately $30,000 per year. These expenses do not include a salary or fee for the advisor, nor do they include most of the distribution or advertising costs. Doing some simple arithmetic, the fund must reach a significant asset size to cover the basic yearly cost (e.g. a 1.2% fee on $2,500,000 of assets would yield $30,000). A much larger base would be needed to cover a fee or salary for the advisor, distribution or advertising costs. As you might suspect, smaller funds, those with relatively small asset bases, need to charge a higher annual fee to be sustainable. On the bright side, from the fund manager's perspective, the rewards for a successful fund can be significant. For instance, a fund with a size of 2 billion dollars with a management fee of 0.7% would provide the fund advisor and her team with an annual 14 million dollars per year to cover the advisor team's salaries and research expenses. Although funds like this exist, many more funds appear to provide less than 2 million dollars per year in fee revenue, due to factors such as a smaller overall asset size or management fee percentage. How do asset management fees impact the investor?

In order to appreciate the impact of asset management fees from an investor's perspective, there are two important considerations. First, how does the fee impact the long-term return to the investor? Second, what is the likelihood that a higher fee will be offset by a better return, thus making the fee irrelevant?

In order to illustrate the long-term impact, I find a helpful measurement is to compare the annual fee to the 4% financial planning rule of thumb you may have heard about. Although not perfect, a long-standing rule of thumb is that, if prudently invested, your nest egg at the start of retirement should be able to support you during a 30-year retirement if you withdraw not much more than 4% of the balance, in current dollars (i.e. appropriately adjusted for inflation), per year. Therefore, it stands to reason that if you pay a 2% annual fee on your nest egg to your investment advisor, you are initially sharing 50% of your nest egg's financial value with, presumably, a very attentive investment advisor. If you pay a 1% annual fee, then you are initially sharing 25% of the amount you are planning to use that first year of retirement. (If you have not already realized it, you now understand why I think you should be interested in low fee investing.) Note that I stated "initially" sharing since, in all fairness, the percentage would eventually go down somewhat as your resulting portfolio balance drops due to withdrawals of money to cover your living expenses and the impact of inflation. The long term effect is not that far off from stated values, however, since you have forever lost the opportunity to invest or enjoy the money spent on fees.

Another way to frame the long-term impact is to look at the opportunity cost of fees over a 35-year accumulation (savings) period. Assuming a 6%

annual return, the opportunity costs are provided in Table 2.

Table 2

Annual Fee	Opportunity Cost
3 %	64 %
2 %	49 %
1 %	28 %
0.2 %	6 %
0.1 %	3 %

For example, $100,000 grows to $768,609 over 35 years at a 6% annual growth rate. With a 2% per year fee, the same $100,000 grows only 4% annually to $394,610 over the same 35-year period.

Note that, at the 2% annual fee level, the 49% opportunity cost over a 35-year accumulation (saving) period is comparable to the 50% initial value noted for the 30-year retirement (spending) scenario.

You may be asking, "How would any rational person provide such a large payment to his investment advisor or believe that his circumstances warrant such a high level of service?" Numerous prospective clients have told me that they do not currently pay for investment advice, or that a 1% or 2% fee does not sound like that much and that everyone needs to make a living. I have observed that fees are often communicated in a way analogous to how a magician's trick works – basically, misdirection of attention. As a non-magician, it fascinates me how an even modestly skilled magician can appear to work miracles before my eyes by directing my attention away from the action that makes the illusion work. In the area of investment fees, the investor's attention is directed to the return and the fee is not placed into any context, except that of a relatively low, seemingly harmless, number. The true context (long-term percentage of your total investment portfolio value) is typically hidden from view. In my opinion, it should come down to how much service you need and what you can afford. Even if fees are bundled with other related services such as tax planning, insurance planning, etc., there still has to be a limit. In so many other areas of life, we all make choices as to what we think we can afford, and use cost to define where we fit in (e.g. first class or coach, cruise or camping, private or public college…). My own experience and observation is that too many investors are paying for a private jet when they do not even need to fly to get to their destination.

In order to provide emphasis, throughout this book I express fees as "per year" rather than dropping the implied expression. When a fee is expressed as 2% instead of 2% per year, it diminishes the significant point that 2% times the number of years grows to a disturbingly large amount of wealth transferred from the investor to the financial service provider.

Financial Planning

Since the best investment advice is typically offered in the context of a broader financial plan, it is important to consider how each of the three service models work as it impacts the fee you are paying, directly or indirectly, and the value you are receiving.

In the hourly, fee-only model, investors with relatively simple or well-defined financial circumstances may require only a minimal planning effort. A fee range based upon 1 to 3 hours of effort, may be all that is needed to set the stage for an appropriate investment recommendation. Investors with more substantial portfolios (e.g. 50% or more of the way towards their financial independence goal) are likely to require a more comprehensive planning effort to assure that the investment advice takes place in the appropriate context (i.e. tax planning, risk management). A fee range based on between 8 and 15 hours of effort, for an initial plan, would be typical. Very large (e.g. over 2 million dollars) or complex portfolios may require more time and effort. Note that annual financial planning expenses tend to be significantly less with each passing year, unless financial circumstances require a significant new amount of effort.

In the assets under management (AUM) fee model it is possible that the financial plan will be provided as part of the ongoing management fee. Some advisors charge separate fees for financial planning and asset management to recognize the potential imbalances that could occur, since the initial planning efforts are typically greater and often simplify with the passage of time. Note that it is important to understand the total annual fees that are being paid. If an advisor charges a 0.5% annual fee to manage a portfolio of mutual funds[1] that charge an annual fee of 0.5%, the total annual fee the investor pays is actually 1.0%. If an advisor charges a 1.0% annual fee to manage a portfolio of actively managed mutual funds[1] that charge an annual fee of 1.0%, the total annual fee the investor pays is actually 2.0%.

The commission-based model also may, or may not, assess a separate fee for the financial planning effort associated with the investment advice and management. Examples will be provided in the next chapter to illustrate how this and the other models may be used in implementing a socially responsible investing strategy. The value of any financial planning activity included in the commission and annual fee, for this model, also needs to take into account the portfolio size, as the examples will show.

Footnote 1 – Note that mutual fund fees (i.e. the expense ratio) typically do not include the fund's internal brokerage and trading costs. The actual investment costs to the investor, therefore, may be more than expected.

CHAPTER 2

CHOOSING AN INVESTMENT APPROACH

Now that the fees have been covered to a sufficient level, you are ready to assess how to use this knowledge to establish an investment approach that meets your needs and is sustainable.   I personally believe that the SRI industry has grown sufficiently large that the needs of many investors can be efficiently met.   In this chapter I would like to provide, by example, several approaches that may be used so that you may identify the category that best works for you.   Since investment offerings do change with time, it is not helpful for me to be too specific in regards to fund or stock names but I will attempt to provide sufficient detail so that you, along with an advisor that is reasonably familiar with SRI, are able to develop a strategy that best meets your current needs.

The following three sections and sub-sections are based on the overall size of your investment portfolio and are intended to stand independently – please pardon the redundancy.

Investor of Modest Means

Perhaps you are just starting out (or not) and would like to know how you might be able to invest $10,000 that represents funds that you are investing for the long term (let us presume you already have an emergency fund in cash, CDs, etc.). Here are some scenarios:

A) You would like to make sure you achieve benchmark market returns (e.g. S&P 500) and do not have a strong need for screening your investments. One low fee approach would be to invest in a low-cost "non-SRI" index fund with a low fee custodian (annual cost typically less than 0.2 percent per year, or in your case, $20 per year). Of course, you might make a few donations to your favorite causes that further advance your worldview and not rely on your investments to help you do this.

B) You would like to make socially responsible investments and need some help. You visit your bank or credit union, and are introduced to their brokerage service provider. They help you identify a fund that meets your objectives. You will typically find that there will be a 5% (approximate) sales charge applied along with an annual fee of 1% per year (approximate). The cost here is $500 initially and $100 per year. Assuming no changes (i.e. new sales charges generated, same portfolio value), your average fee remains $100 per year.

C) You would like to make socially responsible investments and need some help, but do not like the idea of a sales charge, and search out a fee-only advisor who charges based on percent of assets. Based on an average annual fee of 1% per year, you find that you are having a hard time finding someone to work for $100 per year (but maybe you do find someone who recognizes your potential or simply just wants to work with you).

D) You would like to make socially responsible investments and need some help, but would like to offer some "sweat equity" and establish investment accounts with discount brokerage houses with a minimum of guidance. You find a fee-only advisor who works on an hourly basis and has no minimums. You find that he has to spend some time with you to understand your goals and you probably find that your initial cost is less than $500 to identify a low fee SRI passive or actively-managed (no front load or sales charge) with an annual fee between $20 and $100 per year, depending upon your investment objective.

Investor with $200,000 Account Size

You have been investing for a while or just received a windfall. You are not happy with your current investment situation and are considering how you might be able to invest $100,000 in stocks/equities. You know your tolerance for risk and want to have $100,000 in cash, CDs and low fee, short term bond funds (by the way, keep in mind that there are SRI approaches for cash and bonds, but that is a topic for another day). You are investing for the long term. Here are some scenarios:

A) You would like to make sure you achieve benchmark market returns (e.g. S&P 500) and do not have a strong need for screening your investments. One low fee approach would be to invest in a low cost index fund with a low fee custodian (annual cost typically less than 0.2 percent per year or in your case, $200 per year). Of course, you make a few donations to your favorite causes that further advance your worldview.

B) You would like to make socially responsible investments and need some help. You visit your bank or credit union and are introduced to their brokerage service provider. They help you identify a fund or group of actively managed mutual funds that meet your objectives. You will typically find that there will be a 5% (approximate) sales charge applied along with an annual fee of 1% per year (approximate). The sales charge may be significantly lower (e.g. 3%) if you invest in a single fund family, since you will likely qualify for a breakpoint discount which is based on account size. The cost here is up to $5,000 initially and $1,000 per year. Assuming no changes (i.e. no new sales charges generated, same portfolio value), your average fee remains $1,000 per year.

C) You would like to make socially responsible investments and need some help, but do not like the idea of a sales charge and search out a fee only advisor who charges based on percent of assets. Based on an average annual fee of 1% per year, you find that you are having a hard time finding someone to work for about $1,000 per year using this business model, but eventually find someone that recognizes your potential or simply just wants to work with you and will help identify a mutual fund or two to meet your needs.

D) You would like to make socially responsible investments and need some help, but would like to offer some "sweat equity" and establish investment accounts with discount brokerage houses with a minimum of guidance. You find a fee-only advisor who works on an hourly basis and has no minimums. You find that he has to spend some time with you to understand your goals and probably find that your initial cost is less than $1,000 to identify a low fee SRI passive or actively-managed fund (no front load or sales charge) with an annual fee between $200 and $1,000 per year, depending upon your investment objective. It is likely that an investment mix that takes into account your needs will contain a mix of both SRI and non-SRI funds and specific advice on your overall portfolio will be included.

E) You have just read a book on low fee socially responsible investing and liked the chapter on ultra-low fee SRI where you can be more specific about your investment preferences and still obtain the benefits of low cost (see Chapter Four). You find that you have to spend some time with an advisor who is familiar with this approach and that your initial cost is likely to be less than $1,000; your annual cost thereafter is likely to be less than $1,000. Better yet, the annual cost will not increase as your portfolio grows in size. You like the idea of investing in a portfolio of companies that reflect your worldview and are comfortable with the 1% (approximate) per year fee (i.e. ($1,000/$100,000) x 100 = 1%).

Investor with $1,000,000 Account Size

You are well on your way, or have achieved financial freedom. You are not in a position to establish a foundation to support your worldview, but would like to consider how you might be able to invest $500,000 in stocks/equities. You know your tolerance for risk and want to have $500,000 in cash, CDs and low-fee, short-term and medium-term bond funds (as noted earlier, keep in mind that there are SRI approaches for cash and bonds). You are investing for the long term. Here are some scenarios:

A) You would like to make sure you achieve benchmark market returns (e.g. S&P 500) and do not have a strong need for screening your investments. One low fee approach would be to invest in a low-cost index fund with a low fee custodian (annual cost typically less than 0.2 percent per year or in your case, $1,000 per year). Of course, you make generous donations to your favorite causes that further advance your worldview.

B) You would like to make socially responsible investments and need some help. You visit your bank or credit union and are introduced to their brokerage service provider. Or perhaps, you met a financial advisor at a free dinner and seminar on investing. She helps you identify a fund or group of actively managed mutual funds that meet your objectives. You will typically find that breakpoint discounts will be significant due to the size of your account and may be able avoid most sales charges. Any sales charges, along with an annual fee of 1% (approximate) will still apply. The cost may be very high if you do not qualify for breakpoint discounts (i.e. Initial costs could be as high as $25,000 if you have investments placed at various custodians and do not take advantage of breakpoint discounts). Assuming no changes (i.e. new sales charges generated, same portfolio value) or negotiated fee reductions, your average fee remains $5,000 per year. More comprehensive financial planning (e.g. taxes, insurance needs) may or may not be included in the initial price.

C) You would like to make socially responsible investments and need some help, but do not like the idea of a sales charge and search out a fee-only advisor who charges based on percent of assets. Based on an average annual fee of 1% per year, you easily find someone to work for about $5,000 per year. Having read Chapter One, you understand her interest in managing your fixed income account as well. More comprehensive financial planning may or may not be included in the annual fee.

D) You would like to make socially responsible investments and need some help and are willing to offer some "sweat equity" and establish investment accounts with a discount brokerage house with a minimum of guidance. You find a fee-only advisor that works on an hourly basis and has no minimums. You find that she has to spend some time with you to understand your goals; you probably find that your initial cost is less than $1,000 to identify a low fee SRI passive or actively-managed (no front load or sales charge) with an annual fee between $1,000 and $5,000 per year, depending upon your investment objective and choice of funds. It is likely that an investment mix that takes into account your needs will contain a mix of both SRI and non-SRI funds, and specific advice on your overall investment portfolio will be included. An "all SRI" portfolio may require additional effort, depending upon the investment objectives. Add $1,000 or $2,000 to the initial year fee if more comprehensive financial planning is included.

E) You have just read a book on low-fee socially responsible investing and liked the chapter on ultra low-fee SRI where you can be more specific about your investment preferences and still obtain the benefits of low cost (see Chapter Four). You find that you have to spend some time with an advisor who is familiar with this approach; your initial cost is likely to be less than $1,000 and your annual cost, thereafter, is likely to be less than $1,000. Better yet, the annual cost will not increase as your portfolio continues to grow in size. At your current account size, you realize that you are paying up to 0.2% per year. You like the idea of investing in a portfolio of companies that reflect your worldview and find that the low fee of 0.2% per year is attractive. Add $1,000 or $2,000 to the initial year fee if more comprehensive financial planning is included.

Summary

Table three (3) summarizes the approximate investment expenses associated with the various investment approaches described in this chapter. It is clear to see that the commission model may become increasingly costly as the amount invested increases unless significant breakpoint discounts are obtained. A direct comparison of the AUM and hourly model is complicated by the underlying fees of the active or passive strategies that are being used. If you consider the total fee for the approach you want to compare, the illustration can be made more accurate. The hourly model fees in the table were based on a 50/50 mix of passive and active managed funds while the AUM model fees were based on a 1% total annual fee which is available but not necessarily typical. Note that the ultra-low fee model approaches the do-it-yourself approach as the amount invested grows.

Table 3

Invested Amount versus Initial Year Cost (Annual Cost)

	Amount Invested	$10,000	$100,000	$500,000
A	Do-It-Yourself	$20 ($20)	$200 ($200)	$1,000 ($1,000)
B	Commission	$600 ($100)	$3,000 or more ($1,000)	$5,000 or more ($5,000)
C	Assets Under Management (AUM)	N/A	Probably N/A or $1,000 ($1,000)	$5,000 ($5,000)
D	Hourly	$560 ($60)	$1,600 ($600)	$4,000 ($3,000)
E	Ultra-Low Fee	N/A	$1,000 ($1,000)	$1,000 ($1,000)

.

CHAPTER 3

IMPLEMENTATION

Now that you have a better idea of what the lay of the land is regarding fees and investment approaches consistent with those fees, you are in a position to consider implementation.

Using a Broker (Bank, Credit Union Brokerage, Insurance Company, Full Service Brokerage Firm)

As you have seen from the illustrations, this may be a convenient choice for an investor with a relatively modest account size. For larger and larger account sizes, the math suggests that you believe you are still getting services in alignment with the investment cost. Also, you need to keep in mind what you can afford. For instance, many younger investors have more time than money and routinely choose to take on more do-it-yourself home improvement projects, mow their own lawns, wash their cars, and file their own income tax forms. As folks accumulate more wealth and/or have less time than money, it becomes understandable to hire others to perform more and more tasks. I recommend you judge the services of your financial service provider with comparable scrutiny. *Of course, if your belief is that you have identified an investment advisor who can predict the future, no fee is too big.*

Note, also, that your investment choices will typically be more limited when using a service provider who is associated with a given fund family or group of fund families.

Typically, when you invest with a broker, you will have minimum work to do. In the best situation, you will work with someone who fills out most of the paperwork, be placed in an investment that suits your needs and obtain satisfactory results.

Using an Investment Advisor on Fee-Only Basis, Based on Account Size

Depending upon the service levels provided, this may be an appropriate choice for relatively wealthy investors. Of course, all fees should be considered, as they are additive. If an advisor is managing an account that consists of mutual funds that charge their own fee, you need to be aware that it is the total fee that should be considered. For instance, a 0.5% annual fee to the advisor recommending funds that charge their own average fee of 1.0% per year, represents a 1.5% fee annually to you. Being aware of this math, fee-only advisors often reduce their fees in proportion to total asset size. If you have a relatively complex financial life and can benefit from a significant amount of tax and estate planning, along with investment advice, you should take into consideration all of the services provided. If you are an investor who needs to meet frequently with her advisor, in person or over the phone, you should also consider the total amount of service you are receiving.

Be aware that the choice of investments may be limited by the custodian used by the investment advisor.

Using an Investment Advisor on an Hourly, Fee-Only Basis

One of the biggest benefits of paying an advisor by the hour is that you are in control of how much service you choose to buy. It is easy to avoid overpaying for services that you do not need. In implementing an SRI strategy, you can choose among the broader universe of SRI investments, as most hourly advisors do not insist that you have your assets with a specific custodian of assets (i.e. discount brokerage firm). When using an advisor who charges by the hour, it is important to recognize that, unless you pay a retainer fee based on the amount of time involved, your investment portfolio is not being monitored unless you direct the advisor to do so. If your expectation is that your advisor can and should be reacting to frequent market movements, and be in a position to make frequent trades, then you should not use an hourly, fee-only advisor. The hallmark of passive investing strategies is to avoid market timing and frequent rebalancing. Also, note that many advisors who charge on a basis of commissions or asset size do not necessarily rebalance frequently, nor react to world events (knowing that they cannot predict the future either). Using an hourly, fee-only advisor may require more work on your part when it comes to implementation of investment recommendations. Most hourly advisors I know will provide as much help as needed and the amount of time, and resulting investor cost, is typically limited (it is not really that hard with a little guidance). Note that hourly advisors typically do not have authority to access your account and make changes. This places you in control as to when implementation occurs, with or without their help. The cost savings comes at a price – you cannot blame your advisor for bad timing if you control the timing. Again, it should be all about your view of the world.

In using any of the three financial service models, it is important for you to keep in mind that financial planning and investment management each offer you value and the fees you pay for these services should be viewed as independently as possible. This will help you determine what is best for you. All three service models bundle financial planning and investment management, to some degree, and it is helpful to look at them as related, but separate, activities. For instance, financial planning can offer you significant benefits versus the fee paid (e.g. identifying a better pension election or Social Security benefit strategy, identify tax planning actions that can save unnecessary taxes, identifying risk management strategies related to the use of insurance and investment risk, identifying better education funding options, and identifying estate planning strategies to maintain family wealth). Some financial services providers offer financial planning as a part of investment management services. Both services can, and do, contribute significantly to your financial well-being. It would not be difficult for most financial planners to provide examples of when they have saved their clients large amounts of money, far in excess of any fees they charged. *Returning to the transportation analogy, the limousine driver, taxi driver and certified mechanics should be provided a fair wage for their professional services. They do not, however, have a valid claim to a large portion of your wealth simply because they got you safely to your destination.*

CHAPTER 4

ULTRA-LOW FEE SRI

As noted in the introduction, I wanted to find a SRI solution to address the need of a specific group of investors for as low a fee as possible. In most endeavors, any degree of customization would typically lead only to higher cost approaches.

Investment costs are primarily dependent upon research costs, ongoing management costs and distribution/advertising costs. Therefore, an optimum solution would minimize these costs. This chapter examines how each cost was addressed.

Research Cost

As noted earlier there is no shortage of established mutual funds in the SRI world. Also, there is an increasing number of SRI indices (benchmarks) being established with the aim of being investable at a low fee along the lines of a traditional index fund. Mutual funds are required to publish their holdings periodically, and commercially available databases, routinely used by advisors, contain the tools to easily determine the holdings of any particular mutual fund or index fund. It is a relatively simple exercise, therefore, to generate a list of common holdings across a multitude of funds. Since the primary driver of a stock price is supply and demand, a reasonable starting point for low-cost research would be to explore what stock holdings are the most popular among a large group of funds that share similar social screening objectives.

Online databases offer other screening criteria that I believe would be of interest to investors interested in expressing their world outlook even more explicitly through their investment choices. One of the most intriguing possibilities to me was to construct a portfolio that also took into consideration the political accountability of a particular company. The Center for Political Accountability (CPA) publishes a database that provides helpful information in the design of an investment portfolio model addressing the needs of investors, faith-based or otherwise, interested in this screening criteria (**www.politicalaccountability.net**). As illustrated in Chapter 6, other information sources can be used to take additional factors of interest to an investor into consideration.

In order to further keep costs low, I decided to limit the size of the portfolio to between 35 and 50 individual stocks and use a simple decision table (see Chapter 6, Table 4) to determine an initial weighting of 1%, 2% or 3%. The most complex math involved was having one criterion that would be flexible enough to allow the total to be exactly 100%. Research would be limited to using databases that one has authorized access to, asking appropriate questions of the investor, doing some simple math, and testing out the resulting SRI portfolio using available tools to assess its place in investor's the overall portfolio.

Ongoing Management Cost

A portfolio consisting of not more than 50 individual stocks can be managed in several ways. Based on my attraction to passively-managed investments and the desire to minimize the downside effects of an overly-managed/traded portfolio, I would propose that the best use of the portfolio generated for the purpose of ultra-low fee SRI be altered only about once per year. By altered, I mean that the original criteria used to generate the portfolio be re-run and rebalanced or modified, as needed. If the investor would like a new or modified screen to be considered, this would also be a possibility.

I believe the 50-stock portfolio could be used successfully on several low-fee platforms. Integration with an investor's other investments and his advisor's familiarity with the platform should be considered. As an example of how low fee implementation can be achieved, let us take a look at how an hourly advisor would implement this on the Folio Investing® retail platform (note that some advisors would find the same utility using the Folio Investing® Institutional platform). The advisor would provide the investor with a list of up to 50 stocks with weightings of 1%, 2% or 3% and work with him, as needed, to assemble a Watch Portfolio®. The annual flat fee cost for unlimited trades using this platform is currently $290 per year. Also, the platform allows an investor to buy fractional shares of the portfolio constructed, and purchase and sell the entire portfolio in a manner somewhat similar to buying or selling a mutual fund (from the investor's perspective, at least). Given the flat fee, the math needed to calculate ongoing management cost is easy, noting that the hourly advisor does not log any additional billable hours until requested to assist in a reassessment and rebalance.

The largest cost for utilizing this approach is likely to come from the original construction cost. If it is determined that more than one investor is interested in the same criteria and subsequent portfolio model, this cost would be reduced or eliminated for those investors choosing to use an existing model. In many cases, much of the effort will focus on establishing that the financial needs and objectives of the investor are met. Importantly, the fiduciary obligation for the advisor is to assure that the investor is aware of how this portfolio works into his overall investment mix, tax profile, time horizon, and tolerance for risk. The key consideration is that the advisor makes it clear to the investor that the portfolio model is a passive model and requires the investor to arrange for periodic (e.g. annual) evaluation and rebalancing instructions.

Distribution Cost / Advertising

I mentioned earlier that there are a number of costs associated with development and maintenance of a mutual fund approach to investing. In order for a fund to achieve the benefits of scale, inevitably they must be marketed to a large enough audience in order to attract sufficient assets. These costs get passed along to the investor. An ultra-low-fee portfolio has essentially no distribution and advertising cost.

CHAPTER 5

QUESTIONS AND ANSWERS

Here are some anticipated questions and corresponding answers regarding the ultra-low fee approach.

1. A portfolio of 35 to 50 stocks selected in the described manner does not seem representative of any existing index and performance cannot be easily benchmarked. Is this a problem?

This is true, but keep in mind that your worldview is the primary consideration and that you should be prepared to use this approach completely or, in part, in accordance with your investment objective. This is one of the primary reasons why I believe you should use this approach with the assistance of an advisor who can review the proposed portfolio in the full context of your financial position, in the same way as they would look at any other collection of stocks you may own. Historically, and still to this day, there are numerous individual investors holding portfolios consisting of even fewer stocks that may or may not reflect their social preferences. Many popular stocks in SRI portfolios are those of very large companies (large cap stocks). A significant number of stocks are even part of the 30-stock Dow Jones Industrial Average (the Dow), and it is likely that most portfolios generated will consist of stocks of large and mid-sized companies which have a tendency to track two of the most popular indices, the Dow and the S&P 500. Again, the primary purpose of the portfolio is to reflect your worldview.

2. Will a portfolio designed with a potentially large number of minimally tested screening criteria behave unpredictably and be harmful to my finances?

Although my experience with ultra-low fee portfolios developed to date does not indicate unusual behavior as they tend to track the overall market, it is indeed possible that you could choose a set of criteria that results in a portfolio that may produce disappointing results. I believe the role of the advisor, in this instance, would be to help you utilize the portfolio generated or to make agreeable modifications to try to regulate the performance to acceptable levels versus overall market expectations. You and your advisor would jointly review appropriate historical data for the proposed portfolio based on standard analytical tools. More importantly, the portfolio could be watched for a mutually agreed upon period of time before a single dollar is invested, to improve the likelihood of satisfactory performance.

3. Will the fact that the portfolio is dollar-weighted place performance at a disadvantage relative to market-weighted portfolios?

Since the portfolio contains a relatively small number of stocks, there is a balance to be struck between tracking the overall market and the safety provided by limiting the maximum percentage to one single stock to not more than 3.0%. This approach assumes that there is some additional downside protection obtained by using a base grouping of stocks that are very popular holdings in a collection of very large SRI portfolios. It may take many years of experience with this model to establish the validity of this assumption.

4. What are the risks of maintaining a portfolio that is not actively managed?

As noted earlier in Chapter One, there appears to be significant risk when using actively managed portfolios due to the fee drag that occurs. Also, any legally obtained company news that could impact a stock price is not likely to be successfully acted upon by an active fund manager, in that their timing would have to be immediate and correct, in the long-term. If you have a positive view of active management, it would be better for you to be introduced to one of the many actively managed funds that are available. If you are aware of a fair amount of the academic and published data that supports passive management, yet have a strong desire for having your investments reflect your worldview, than the ultra-low fee approach should be of interest to you, provided that you have investable assets of sufficient size to make the approach worthwhile.

5. Will an investor-defined portfolio make it difficult for an investment advisor to structure an overall portfolio that is considered well-balanced?

The diversity of managed portfolios that are already available make it difficult to define "well-balanced". If you and your advisor are more concerned with theoretical portfolio balance at just about any cost, this approach is not for you. If you are comfortable with a less rigid approach to portfolio construction, you may want to study this option to determine if a certain significant reduction in investment expense more than offsets the potential theoretical impact of some imbalance. Of course, both you and your advisor should consider appropriate ways to achieve reasonable balance, at a reasonable cost, by partially utilizing other low fee funds.

6. How would I find an advisor willing to utilize this approach?

There are investment advisors across the country and world who upon reading this short book, would understand how to implement this approach to socially responsible investing (Chapter Six goes into more detail). There may be some advisors willing to implement this approach, but who may not want to be bothered with the portfolio construction process. In this instance, they can subcontract the portfolio construction to an advisor interested in this work. I am already aware of a number of fellow members of the Garrett Planning Network who are interested in this portfolio development approach, as it would fit well with their hourly fee-only practice. I would anticipate that other fee-only advisors outside of the Garrett Planning Network® would be willing to provide this service, provided their business model or practice allows them to offer it.

7. How can low portfolio cost be assured, since advisors have a wide range of fees?

There is no absolute assurance that you will be able to find an advisor who is willing to embrace this low-fee model. Also, your worldview may prove to be too restrictive to allow for efficient construction. I base the "less than $1,000" construction cost on the experience I have had to date. The construction process is relatively simple and one that can be mastered in a short period of time. It is hoped that market forces will be at work, and an increasing number of advisors will become proficient at this approach and not keep the availability of this service a secret.

8. How can low maintenance cost be assured since various discount brokerage firms and investment management firms have different cost structures?

The first step would be to check with your current investment custodian and work with an advisor to determine if you would be able to implement this strategy in a cost-efficient manner, without the inconvenience of having to move some of your assets onto another platform. If this does not work, I have already mentioned one low fee custodian that could be considered (Folio Investing®). Stock trading fees *are under constant pressure downwards and you should be able to find a trading platform that works for you (e.g. a stock portfolio of 50 stocks, traded at $7 per trade, is still only $350 per year, provided that you make purchases or sales only once per year).*

9. If I work with an advisor to generate a portfolio of 50 stocks, is it Okay if I buy them over the course of time or buy only the specific stocks I really like first?

No. This defeats the purpose of diversification and the discipline associated with not trying to time the market on one specific stock over another.

10. Would it be reasonable to buy the portfolio of stocks when the market appears to be undervalued and/or sell the portfolio of stocks when the market appears to be somewhat pricey?

The same discipline that one would apply to buying a mutual fund for the long-term would apply, however, there may be some circumstances where this approach may be warranted (e.g. during periods near rebalancing or tax loss harvesting).

11. Regarding taxes - what are some of the tax considerations for this approach versus a mutual fund investment?

Since this portfolio is a collection of individual stocks rather than a mutual fund, you have a significant advantage over a mutual fund investor in that mutual fund capital gain distributions are not always predictable and within the control of the investor. Though messy in a taxable account (e.g. 50 entries on a Schedule D), this approach would allow for some tax planning. In a tax-deferred account, there is no significant tax planning difference that I am aware of.

12. Is it appropriate to consider constructing and investing in several portfolio models?

As experience is gained with this approach, it is appropriate to consider the use of several models. Additional development work would add to the cost and is not encouraged at the outset. Also, more thorough study would be encouraged to make the resulting portfolio model less volatile and more effective (e.g. a portfolio focused on small company stocks might need to limit allocation maxima to 2% and contain more than 50 stocks as would a model based on a narrow sector such as alternative energy). It should be noted that investment platforms using a flat annual fee could implement multiple models without incurring additional trading expenses.

13. What are the benefits again besides lower investment cost?

Besides the benefits already noted, such as potential tax planning opportunities and aligning your investments with your values, consider the impact on your behavior as an investor. As much as both investors and advisors try to believe they can be immune to emotional reactions to market volatility, there appears to be little evidence to support much success in this regard. Although I make no claim of credentials as a psychologist, it would seem reasonable to expect that you would be more likely to stand firm in volatile times with an investment set representing your worldview than a set of investments to which you have less connection. Of course, it is up to both you and your advisor to ease into this investment approach, so that it becomes a source of firmness, and not uncertainty.

From a standpoint of SRI, one of the common criticisms of mutual fund investing is that there is no assurance that an investor's viewpoint is being represented in any proxy votes that take place in a given company whose stock is being held. This separation of investor and investment has been expressed eloquently by authors, such as Jack Bogle (see references). By holding individual stocks, any proxy voting materials can be directly acted upon by you, the investor. Better yet, however, by holding stock in companies that are screened in accordance with your values, there will likely be fewer controversial proxy issues of concern.

If during the course of time, you become aware of some attributes of a company whose stock you are holding that disturbs you, you have the ability to consider redefining the screening criteria periodically. Rather than being negatively impacted by the unexpected consequences of arbitrary decisions on the selection and purchase timing of individual stocks, changes of investment preferences can be treated in a more systematic manner.

14. Will the low fee approach work for all areas of SRI?

Some focused screens may not be good candidates. For instance, some areas such as clean technology and alternative energy, may be too speculative for this approach, or require a significant amount of research, and care should be taken. Further testing would be needed to determine the amount of diversification that would be appropriate for some portfolio models with a narrow focus.

15. What if I really like the idea of investing per my worldview but do not have enough to invest to make it cost effective?

A closer look at some of the existing low fee exchange traded funds (ETFs) or SRI mutual index funds should be considered.

16. Would there be a significant cost saving if I use an existing portfolio that an advisor has already established to address a given set of values/perspectives?

Yes. This represents an ideal situation and the resulting investment costs would be lower. Note, however, that portfolio documentation should be reviewed by both you and your advisor, to your satisfaction, to ensure that it meets your investment objectives. If you are already working with an advisor utilizing this approach, and choose to direct some of your funds into an existing model, the incremental cost to use this approach would be even lower.

17. How likely is it that a 35- to 50-stock portfolio will track one of the established benchmarks?

In recent history, stock prices of most companies have tended to move up and down together, and a 40- to 50-stock portfolio is likely to provide sufficient correlation to demonstrate a fair amount of market tracking. Given that there are a multitude of indices and benchmarks, I would maintain that attempting to track a given benchmark is, in essence, also akin to taking a worldview position. For instance, you decide that your objective is to track the S&P 500, a large collection of stocks - your worldview is that satisfactory long-term investment performance is defined as capturing the returns of holding a market-weighted basket of stocks representative of a generally accepted approach to measure economic activity. Of course the benchmarks themselves are not fixed and stocks are added and subtracted periodically. It is important to note that the discipline of diversification, limited modifications and periodic rebalancing of the index produces relatively satisfactory results. Any given index does not have a certain claim to superior performance over any other index. Tracking a benchmark is no assurance of positive or superior returns versus any other particular worldview. Therefore, it would appear that the benefit to be obtained is the discipline rather than replication of the allocation represented in the benchmark. It typically takes a very long time to determine which model or benchmark will produce optimal performance. For instance, what does it imply when an active fund manager dismisses his 1- year and 3-year performance data when he is below the benchmark, noting that his 10 year record is over the benchmark? What is the appropriate time horizon to measure performance? From your perspective, it could be your lifetime if you plan on holding the investment and passing it on to heirs. Or it could be until you plan on using the invested funds for something else.

18. What if the "sin" stocks outperform the benchmarks over the long-term?

If this occurs over the time horizon of interest, you would have been better off financially investing in the "sin" stocks or a fund that contains these stocks. Of course, the future performance of this group or any group of stocks is unknown. It is clear, however, that the popularity of socially responsible investing is steadily growing and that momentum would appear to favor stocks of companies that are aligned with this significant trend.

19. To put fees in perspective, Chapter 1 references a 4% withdrawal rule. Will this rate still apply if economic performance continues to be as poor as the last decade?

There has been more discussion recently in the financial planning community about the potential need to revise the withdrawal rate down significantly (e.g. 3%). This implies that fee control will become even more important if investors are to reach their goals.

CHAPTER 6

FOR ADVISORS

Although investors are encouraged to read this chapter, this information is geared toward the advisor.

The portfolio construction process starts with reviewing a questionnaire completed by the investor or a representative of a group of investors.

The questionnaire should be designed to allow the advisor to most easily match existing SRI mutual funds with suitable candidates should an investor choose the convenience of direct investment in mutual funds. If a more customized portfolio is desired, then the initial groups of stocks can be identified using a list of common holdings. A typical questionnaire might include the tables provided on the following pages.[1]

Issue	No Screen (X)	Seek Positive Action (X)
Climate Change		
Clean Technology		
Pollution		
Environment		

Issue	No Screen (X)	Avoid Investment (X) in Bad Actors	Seek Positive Action (X)
Pollution			
Diversity			
Human Rights			
Labor Relations			
Executive Pay			

Issue	No Screen (X)	Avoid Investment (X) in Bad Actors	Exclude Investment (X)
Alcohol			
Animal Testing			
Defense/Weapons			
Gambling			
Tobacco			

Issue	Positively Weight Good Actors (X), Comment or Avoid Investment In ___
Corporate Political Transparency	
Corporate Non-Partisanship	
100 Best/Worst Companies for Social Criteria X	
100 Best/Worst Companies for Social Criteria Y	
Other __	
Other __	

It is important that the questions link to source data that both the investor and advisor accept as viable. As more advocates of social causes develop the resources to publish their findings and maintain their listings, socially conscious investors will be able to translate this information into action by targeting their investments accordingly.

By using a simple, yet methodical, approach to the portfolio construction process, experienced investors and advisors will be in a position to reduce the "fee drag" associated with more complex methodologies This approach may make socially responsible investing attractive to a wider audience. Time will tell how these portfolios perform. It is important for the advisor to assess the risks, communicate them to the investor and offer advice based upon the investor's best interest.

As noted previously, the first step involves identifying a core list of popular stocks that are used by existing mutual funds which are in alignment with the investor's interest, as stated on the questionnaire. Any suitable source of mutual fund screening criteria may be used provided that you have approved access to the information. The US Social Investment Forum (**www.ussif.org**) publishes a particularly helpful document on its website, consisting of a very comprehensive list of SRI mutual funds and the associated screening criteria used by each fund.

In order to help assure that the most popular stocks are going to rise to the top of the list, it is important to consider the size of the potential funds under study. Admittedly, some good investments may be overlooked. The popular stocks are, however, more widely held and, if socially responsible investing continues to take a larger share of investable dollars, will continue to be in demand. In looking at the list of potential funds, note that the list can be further reduced by eliminating funds that differ only in their fee classification (e.g. investor, institutional).

After at least ten funds have been identified, construct a portfolio containing approximately equal weighting of each of the funds using whatever portfolio tool is at your disposal. Again, use your portfolio analysis tool to generate a list of common holdings listed in order of relative portfolio weighting (this order will come in handy as it will rank the most popular holdings). If you do not have access to a portfolio analysis tool, it is still possible to manually collect lists of publicly disclosed holdings for the mutual funds of interest. As a reference point, it may be helpful to include a social index fund as one or more of the funds to guide your judgment.

The next step will be to populate the table (Table 4) which will be used to consider additional criteria. Using the additional criteria, add a +1, -1, or x 0 as defined.

Low Fee Socially Responsible Investing

Table 4

Stock Ticker	Crit. A	Crit. B	Crit. C	Crit. D	Crit. E	Crit. F	Crit. G	Total	x 0	Allocate
ABC	+1			+1		+1	+1	4		3 %
DEF	+1		+1				+1	3		3 %
GHI	+1					+1	+1	3		3 %
JKL	+1	+1					+1	3		3 %
MNO	+1		+1					2		2 %
PQR	+1		+1					2		2 %
STU	+1		+1	+1		+1		4		3 %
VWX	+1			+1	- 1			1	x 0	0 %
⋮										

Note that Table 4 provides a typical example and each portfolio development worksheet is likely to differ somewhat. Note that only the top of the table is illustrated and the number of rows will typically reflect about 50 individual stocks.

Criteria A - (+1) One of the top 50 stocks which are used by at least two different mutual fund families that screen for criteria important to the investor, listed in order of popularity/weight.

Criteria B - (+1) Listed as a company that prohibits spending corporate cash on politics per the Center for Political Accountability:
www.politicalaccountability.net

Criteria C - (+1) Listed on the 100 Best Companies List for social criteria X per specified online source.

Criteria D - (+1) Listed on the 100 Best Companies List for social criteria Y per specified online source.

Criteria E - (-1) Investor preference is to underweight stocks in the financial sector.

Criteria F - (+1) Listed as one of the top 10 companies on the S&P 100 in the area of political accountability and transparency per the Center for Political Accountability:
www.politicalaccountability.net

Criteria G - (+1) From top to bottom of list, add +1 until total reaches 100, as needed, to weight the more popular stocks in the initial sorting and obtain a total of 100.

x 0 - indicate "times zero" for any other criteria that would exclude this holding based on any listed criteria where investment is to be avoided (e.g. avoid any stock with a financial rating below an agreed upon value, using a commercially available rating source).

Note that the maximum initial allocation allowed by the model is 3%.

It is possible that in some cases it will not be practical to accommodate an investor as his criteria and preferences may not translate to a reasonably objective set of sorting criteria. Also, if public or commercially available data are not available for a specific social concern, it is out of the scope of this simple tool to incorporate it in the model development.

After obtaining a list of stocks and % allocation values, the next step is to evaluate the portfolio as you would evaluate any other portfolio. With the familiar caveat that past performance is not reflective or a guarantee of future returns, you are now able to make a determination how this portfolio might be useful in the overall portfolio of the investor.

It is recommended that you monitor the performance of the portfolio prior to recommending investment in it. As noted earlier, there need be no urgency to use this tool as a primary means of identifying investment of real dollars until both you and the investor become comfortable with the model. The amount of transition time is likely to vary. More seasoned investors will likely become comfortable in less time, as they will have significant experience in weighing the long-term implications of minimal fee drag and not expect the portfolio to have immediate or certain performance benefits.

In time, you will find which screening criteria are most popular with investors and accumulate, potentially, a growing list of helpful criteria. In order to assimilate this information into the model building process, it is recommended that you update the questionnaire accordingly.

After you have developed the portfolio model and have data available to share with the investor, it is recommended that you also share a draft investment policy statement (see Chapter 8). If you are providing advice on the entire portfolio, then the SRI portfolio should be treated in the appropriate context.

It is anticipated that, as interest and use of this portfolio modeling tool grows, there will be opportunities to share models, newly identified data sources and insights regarding making improvements to the tool, while still keeping it simple and cost-effective. We have reserved a domain name as a potential future forum for this activity:

www.lowfeesociallyresponsibleinvesting.com

Footnote 1 – The questionnaire should provide an explanation of the terms used in the table:

No Screen (X) – No strong desire that this criteria be taken into consideration when choosing investments.

Seek Positive Action – Looking to invest in companies that are making strides in a particular area, especially when compared with their peers.

Avoid Investment (X) in Bad Actors – Looking to avoid investment in companies that are poor performers in a particular area when compared with their peers.

Exclude Investment (X) – Want to specifically avoid investment in companies that are involved in a particular industry.

CHAPTER 7

FOR INVESTORS

Here are a few points for the investor to consider.

The portfolio process starts with the questionnaire. More thoughtful responses are likely to result in a screen that better reflects your worldview. Please keep in mind that the results of this process may not meet your expectations. You may expect a tool with more precision or a tool that identifies a wonderful list of companies that define an ideal world. You may be discouraged by the reality that existing screens do not yet detect certain corporate behaviors and attributes, resulting in some companies being screened favorably while not meeting your expectations.

It is hoped you will see the utility of this investment approach and look forward to tracking how more and more companies vie to become listed as "best of class" in the areas of social action that appeal to you.

If you tend to have a worldview consistent with the use of a good tool until the perfect ones come along, then I encourage you to work with someone who can help you translate your views into positive social action. If you believe that collective action of like-minded investors can move society forward, then I would encourage you to determine which approach is best suited to your financial position. Also, I would encourage you to read some of the excellent books on the topic of SRI to identify other ways you can target your financial resources and still obtain a satisfactory return.

If your current account size or risk tolerance does not warrant use of the ultra-low-fee approach, you may still benefit from the use of low fee mutual or exchange traded funds that offer some degree of screening. It is recommended that you discuss the suitability of some potential choices that are available with your advisor. Alternatively, a moderate-fee actively managed fund may be in good alignment with your values and also worthwhile.

Note that the focus of this book is socially responsible investing with the focus on low fees and alignment with an investor's perspective. The cost comparisons provided, were intended to provide sufficient clarity to allow you to determine what is appropriate for your financial circumstances. It is very important to note that investing should be done with the bigger picture in mind. In simple financial situations, establishing the bigger picture does not necessarily require a big investment in time or effort.

As financial circumstances become more complex, it is important that the bigger picture be addressed in order for your investment selections to be placed in the proper context. In seeking to obtain a more comprehensive financial plan, I would recommend that you consider taking comparable care in assessing the value you are getting from your financial planner or advisor, her objectivity and how much you can, or need to, afford. Again, to borrow from an earlier analogy – we do not all need to hire a full-time driver if we only need directions.

CHAPTER 8

INVESTMENT POLICY STATEMENT

A sample investment policy statement (IPS) is provided in this chapter to illustrate how the SRI portfolio model might be handled. Integration with other investments in a given portfolio should be handled appropriately.

Investment Policy Statement

For

General Socially Responsible Investing Portfolio with Emphasis on Political Non-Partisanship and Disclosure

Portfolio Construction Date:_____

Portfolio Recommended Re-evaluation Date:

_____

Investor Name:_____

Advisor Name:_____

Advisor Address:_____

_____

_____

Advisor Signature / Date:_____

Investor Signature / Date:_____

Portfolio Established by:_____

Recommended Custodian:_____

Account Type:_____

Advisor Recommendations/ Use and Implementation

I.   Investment Objectives
        a. The primary objective is to provide an equity portfolio that is consistent with a worldview represented by the title of portfolio.
        b. The portfolio is designed to hold no fewer than 35 and no more than 50 individual stocks at initial allocations of 1%, 2% or 3%. Portfolio dollar weighting is intended to minimize downside risk from extremely poor performance of an individual stock and limit the number of holdings to simplify implementation. A minimum of 35 holdings is intended to provide a reasonable amount of diversification, but there is no intention to represent all market sectors or reflect any established index.
        c. In order to increase the amount of investment return available to you, the portfolio is designed to be implemented with no day-to-day active management cost. Annual re-evaluation and rebalancing is

strongly recommended. This activity requires you to initiate efforts to obtain the latest model revision and work with your advisor to establish that the portfolio continues to be in your best interest.

d. Again, the focus of the investment choices will be to reflect your worldview. Discussion between you and your advisor is necessary to assure that the subject portfolio reflects your objective. If a modified portfolio design is appropriate, you recognize that the cost of portfolio development is your responsibility.

II. Investment Guidelines

a. Time Horizon – In order to reduce trading cost and portfolio management fees, the portfolio is intended to be re-evaluated and rebalanced annually. Portfolio use is, therefore, more consistent with a passive, rather than active, strategy. Investment purchases or sales can occur at anytime, dependent upon the needs or preferences of an individual investor. Some investment platforms will be more suited to incremental investment, while other platforms may present a cost constraint on investment purchase timing. Portfolio rebalancing activity is flexible and should be agreed upon between you and your advisor.

b. Permissible Investments – The portfolio model will include publicly traded stocks. US and international stocks will be included on the basis of the screening process utilized. An initial allocation of a particular stock will be limited to not more than 3%. A minimum initial allocation to a single stock will be 1%.

c. Investment Risk – The amount of acceptable investment in this model is to be determined by you and your advisor on the basis of your investment objectives, risk profile and how best this model may fit into your overall investment portfolio. Data provided to illustrate how this portfolio would have performed historically is intended only to approximate potential risk, and you must recognize that performance may be poor in relation to traditional equity benchmarks.

III. Investment Logistics
   a. Upon approval of the policy, it is up to you to implement on your own or with some assistance from your advisor or custodian.
   b. You should be aware that investment in taxable accounts will require tracking of cost basis information, and appropriate tax planning implications should be taken into consideration. For tax-advantaged accounts, cost basis tracking will typically not be a significant consideration.
   c. You should note the one-year re-evaluation date of the portfolio. You should work with your advisor to obtain the revised allocation and any instructions regarding how to rebalance using your existing custodian.
   d. You should monitor account statements provided by your custodian and contact your advisor with any questions or concerns, especially if your risk profile or investment needs have changed.

IV.   Investment Allocation

   a. Based on the portfolio model of interest, the recommended initial allocation is provided in the following table.   For taxable accounts, it is recommended that dividends and gains are not reinvested. For tax-advantaged accounts, it is generally recommended to reinvest dividends and gains. Your preference is a consideration, and the impact of this decision should be reviewed by both you and your advisor.

Equity	Initial Allocation
Stock ABC	3 %
Stock DEF	3 %
Stock GHI	3 %
Stock JKL	3 %
Stock MNO....	2 %.....

b. Note that the portfolio model is designed to be purchased or sold as a whole and that you should avoid adding or subtracting stock choices or making allocation adjustments. Any reason to do so should open a discussion as to the appropriateness of the model and whether or not changes should be made in a more disciplined fashion.

V. Performance Reporting

a. Commercial tools may be used by the advisor to illustrate approximate portfolio performance based on what information is readily available to the advisor. You should rely on reports from your custodian to monitor your investment performance. The advisor may only be able to produce reports that illustrate performance of the portfolio using time frames built into the software tools she has access to and may not be in a position to determine your actual performance.

b. It should be recognized that, by definition, the primary objective is to invest according to your worldview using a passive strategy designed to keep fees relatively low. Performance may either exceed or underperform traditional benchmark performance in the short, medium or long term. The comfort level that you have with this approach must be considered prior to investment, and you should review your comfort level periodically (e.g. annual re-evaluation or if his financial circumstances change).

c. Reviewed and approved by:

_____

Sample Portfolio Construction Report

Portfolio Title: General Socially Responsible Investing Portfolio with Emphasis on Political Non-Partisanship and Disclosure

Portfolio Construction Date:_____

Portfolio Recommended Re-evaluation Date:

_____

Tom Nowak

Portfolio Established by:_____

_____

_____

Disclaimer: This portfolio was established as a reasonable effort to generate a portfolio model that is consistent with your objectives based on the responses indicated on the questionnaire provided. The portfolio model construction process generates a model based on information that may be out-of-date or even inaccurate as publicly available and reported information is used. The portfolio will not be monitored by anyone since the objective is to produce a portfolio model consistent with a passive buy-and-hold strategy. You maintain responsibility to understand the limitations involved in identifying a socially responsible portfolio that is consistent with your worldview in a cost-efficient manner. It is critical that you understand that the benefits of low portfolio development and implementation cost may not be rewarded in future performance.

Primary Criteria:

1) Exclusion of Alcohol and Tobacco industries is a high priority.

2) Positive impact in the areas of climate, clean technology, the environment, community development and board issues are desirable.

3) Avoidance of defense/weapons industry, gambling and companies involved in significant animal testing is desirable.

4) Corporate non-partisanship and transparency is desirable and favored in the allocation.

5) Corporations recognized on the 100 Best Companies List for social criteria X and Y should be favored in the allocation.

Some relatively large existing mutual funds which are reported in public databases (e.g. **www.ussif.org**) to screen for criteria listed in items 1 through 3, are:

Ticker	Ticker	Ticker
XXXXX	XXXXX	XXXXX
XXXXX	XXXXX	XXXXX
XXXXX	XXXXX	XXXXX
XXXXX	XXXXX	XXXXX

See attachment (*not provided in this example*) for list of the top 50 (approximate) stock holdings of the funds listed.

See table containing stock listing and screening criteria used (*see Chapter Six for example of this table*).

See recommended portfolio allocation and analysis of historical performance illustration (*not provided in this example*). Note that past performance is not a guarantee of future results and that future performance is unknowable.

CHAPTER 9

SUSTAINABLE AND RESPONSIBLE INVESTING

The acronym "SRI" is also used to signify *sustainable and responsible investing* as a potential distinction from socially responsible. For those familiar with this area of investing, there are a quite a number of additional modifiers (e.g. *mission-based*, *green*, *clean tech*). It is my belief that it is important that the investment process, itself, is sustainable and that lower fees and broader access can make a significant contribution toward this goal.

A sustainable investment process should maximize the benefits to the investor and consumer of the capital provided, rather than the intermediary. The recent financial crisis clearly indicated the lack of sustainability of financial services and engineering, themselves, as a significant creator of social wealth. Technology and information abundance can be tools to increase credibility and efficiency of the investment process. As illustrated in Chapter One, it is difficult to imagine the sustainability of an investment process that consumes a significant portion of investor wealth.

For some, criticism of having financial service providers charge "what the traffic may bear" fees may sound anti-capitalistic and an exercise in partisan politics. Any partisanship is not intended. There is general agreement that the strength of sustainable investing is that it can advance a broad range of social purposes. Clearly, the roots of SRI were with faith-based communities and ongoing support is still being provided by these communities. For those looking for justification in charging unnecessarily high fees for their services, they would find little comfort in a serious read of the Holy Books of the world's major religions (e.g. Biblical reference of Christ tossing the money changers out of the temple). Clearly communicating all fees to all investors should provide for more sustainability as well.

Investment returns for the equity investor may be harder and harder to come by in the years and decades ahead as social and private corporations gain market share over their competition (e.g. credit unions versus traditional banks). It should not be surprising if we find that companies that score well in SRI screens will fare much better than their counterparts in this environment. Of course, there is no evidence to support a quick or even likely death of capitalism in the foreseeable future. It is clear, however, that the world's tolerance for unbridled capitalism has worn thin and that socially responsible companies will increasingly find more favor with investors. In investing, one must look at the possibilities and realize that wishful thinking does not contribute to successful investment outcomes in the long term. In order to prepare for the possibilities, placing investments in more sustainable entities would certainly appear less risky, if not more rewarding.

Bibliography

William F. Sharpe, *The Arithmetic of Active Management*, The Financial Analyst, Journal Vol. 47, No.1, January/February 1991. p.7-9

Richard A. Ferri, *The Power of Passive Investing*, Hoboken, New Jersey: John Wiley & Sons, Inc., 2011

Larry E. Swedroe, *The Only Guide to a Winning Investment Strategy You'll Ever Need* , St Martin's Press, 175 Fifth Avenue, New York, NY 10010, 2005

Taylor Larimore, Mel Lindauer, Michael LeBoeuf, *The Bogleheads' Guide to Passive Investing*, Hoboken, New Jersey, John Wiley & Sons, Inc. 2006

John C. Bogle, *The Battle for the Soul of Capitalism*, Yale University Press, New Haven and London, 2005

John C. Bogle, *Enough*, Hoboken, New Jersey, John Wiley & Sons, Inc. 2009

Ann C. Logue, *Socially Responsible Investing for Dummies*, Wiley Publishing, Inc., Hoboken, New Jersey, 2009

Scott J. Budde, *Compelling Returns A Practical Guide to Socially Responsible Investing*, John Wiley & Sons, Inc., 2008

ABOUT THE AUTHOR

Tom Nowak, CFP®, is founder and Principal of Quantum Financial Planning LLC, an hourly, fee-only financial planning and Registered Investment Advisory firm located near Grayslake, Illinois. He is a member of The Garrett Planning Network, Inc., a nationwide network of professional fee-only financial advisors. Founded by Sheryl Garrett, CFP®, members of the Garrett Planning Network share a common goal – to make competent and objective advice accessible through hourly, as-needed financial planning. Tom is also a member of the National Association of Personal Financial Advisors (NAPFA), the largest professional association of comprehensive, fee-only financial planners in the United States. He may be reached at: info@quantumfinancialplanning.com.